# Baby Animals

Marfé Ferguson Delano

NATIONAL
GEOGRAPHIC
KiDS

WASHINGTON, D.C.

# Look, a baby!

Some babies snuggle on snowy sheets of ice.

Some babies cuddle
in warm, cozy dens.

Others live in nests high in trees.

Some babies toddle and trot on grassy hills and plains.

# Splash!

And some swim and leap through wavy seas.

Which would you rather eat: fish, worms, or bugs?

# Feed me!

All baby animals have to eat to grow, just like you. Baby birds gobble up food their parents bring to them, such as tasty bugs or fish.

How wide can you open your mouth?

This bird is bringing its chicks a yummy frog dinner!

Open wide for a delicious bug!

Some baby animals are called mammals. They drink milk from their mother. Bears, cheetahs, and whales are mammals. So are humans.

Let's rub noses! Orca babies stay close to their moms.

How many cheetah cubs do you see in this picture?

This mama bear has three cubs to feed. How many children are in your family?

11

Some baby animals can walk soon after they're born.

Some need a lift
from mom or dad.

13

Boing! Boing! Boing! Can you jump like a wallaby?

# Hang on!

Some babies bounce along, snug in mother's pouch.

Other babies have to hang on tight!

15

# Bath time!

Mother elephants give their babies dust baths! The dirt helps protect their skin.

How do you keep your skin and hair clean?

When you were a baby, your parents kept you neat and clean. They bathed you and washed your hair. Some animal parents keep their babies tidy, too. But you might be surprised by how they do it!

To keep her baby clean, a monkey mom picks dirt and insects off its skin and fur.

A mountain lion mother uses her tongue instead of a washcloth to clean her cub.

How do you think it would feel to be licked by a mountain lion?

17

Baby animals have a lot to learn, from jumping to climbing ...

Baby bears have sharp claws that help them grip tree trunks. Have you ever climbed a tree?

How high can you climb? As high as these baby bears?

19

... from swimming to flying!

What do you think this water feels like? Would you like to swim in it?

Ready, set, flap! This eagle chick is testing its wings, practicing for the day it will fly out of the nest.

21

It's playtime! Some babies swing and scamper through trees.

# Growl!

Some baby animals pretend to fight. They tumble and tussle and wrestle and bite. Pretend fighting helps baby animals learn to hunt!

23

# My turn!

How do you think this baby elephant brings grass to its mouth?

As they grow older, baby animals learn to find food for themselves. Some babies watch and copy their mother as she eats grass, leaves, or fruit.

How high can you stretch your neck? High enough to reach juicy leaves?

Others learn to dig for worms or bugs. Some mother animals teach their babies how to catch fish or hunt.

This young fox caught a mouse dinner all by itself!

Meerkat parents teach their babies how to scratch in the dirt to find insects to eat.

"Hey, Mom, what are we hunting for? Seals again?"

25

The world is full of
things for babies
to explore—to sniff
and touch and taste!

Ah, there's nothing like a sweet-smelling flower! Do you like to smell flowers?

27

# Shhh!

All that learning and playing and exploring can make a baby tired. Baby animals need their sleep—just like you.

# The Name Game!

Some baby animals are called by special names. For example, a baby penguin is called a chick. Baby goats are called kids. Here are some more baby animals, with their special names. Can you say what the grown-up animals are called?

a. Calf

b. Foal

c. Joey

d. Fawn

e. Cub

f. Owlet

Answer key: a. Elephant;
b. Zebra; c. Kangaroo;
d. Deer; e. Lion; f. Owl

# For my wise and beautiful mother, Marie Ferguson
## —MFD

**Editor:** Ariane Szu-Tu
**Art Director:** Amanda Larsen
**Designer:** Callie Broaddus
**Photography Editor:** Lori Epstein

National Geographic supports K–12 educators with ELA Common Core Resources. Visit www.natgeoed.org/commoncore for more information.

Trade paperback ISBN: 978-1-4263-2046-0
Reinforced library binding ISBN: 978-1-4263-2047-7

The publisher gratefully acknowledges zoologist Lucy Spelman, D.V.M., and National Geographic's early childhood development specialist Catherine D. Hughes for their expert review of the book.

Printed in Hong Kong
15/THK/1